READY, SET, CODE!

CODING with Hopscotch

Álvaro Scrivano
Illustrated by Sue Downing

Lerner Publications ◆ Minneapolis

First American edition published in 2019 by Lerner Publishing Group, Inc.

First published in Great Britain in 2018 by Wayland
Copyright © Hodder and Stoughton, 2018
All rights reserved.

Editor: Sarah Silver
Design and illustrations: Collaborate

Lerner Publications Company
A division of Lerner Publishing Group, Inc.
241 First Avenue North
Minneapolis, MN 55401 USA

For reading levels and more information, look up
this title at www.lernerbooks.com.

Main body text set in Frutiger LT Pro 45 Light.
Typeface provided by Linotype AG.

Library of Congress Cataloging-in-Publication Data

Names: Scrivano, Álvaro, 1973– author. | Downing, Sue, 1964– author.
Title: Coding with Hopscotch / Álvaro Scrivano, Sue Downing.
Description: Minneapolis : Lerner Publications, [2019] | Series: Ready, set, code! | Includes bibliographical references and index. | Audience: Ages 7–11. | Audience: Grades 4 to 6.
Identifiers: LCCN 2018029948 (print) | LCCN 2018032119 (ebook) | ISBN 9781541543010 (eb pdf) | ISBN 9781541538740 (lb : alk. paper) | ISBN 9781541546653 (pb : alk. paper)
Subjects: LCSH: Hopscotch (Computer program language)—Juvenile literature. | Microcomputers—Programming—Juvenile literature.
Classification: LCC QA76.7.H57 (ebook) | LCC QA76.7.H57 S38 2019 (print) | DDC 005.1—dc23

LC record available at https://lccn.loc.gov/2018029948

Printed in China
1-45057-35884-7/9/2018

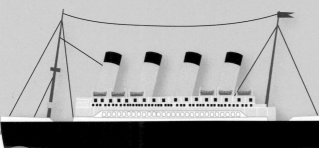

Contents

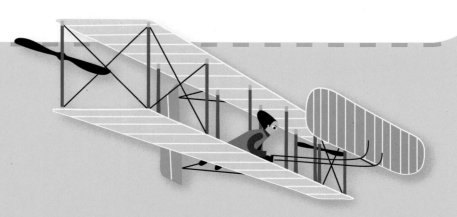

What Is Hopscotch?

Computers can only do what you say, and they will follow your instructions in the order you tell them. Telling a computer what to do is called programming. The person who writes these instructions is called a programmer. You will become a great computer programmer working on the projects in this book!

Hopscotch is a simple programming tool that allows you to create your own computer programs and have a lot of fun.

Note to parents:

The projects in this book require the latest version of Hopscotch on an iPad, iPhone, or iPad mini. You can download Hopscotch for free using this link: https://www.gethopscotch.com.

Make sure your version of Hopscotch is fully up-to-date, or you won't have access to all the code blocks required to work on these projects.

The projects in this book have measurements that work more accurately on iPads. If you are working on an iPad mini or iPhone, you might need to adjust the coordinates and the size of some objects.

Emojis

The projects in this book use emojis. You can download the emoji keyboard by going to Settings on your device.

To add emojis to the project, add a text object instead of a character; then tap the smiley on the keyboard to switch to the emoji menu. Then choose what you want from the menu.

Menu blocks

When you create a new Hopscotch program, you will use some of the blocks below. You will find them in the box that says Add code next to each character you add to your program. When you tap on Add code, four options are displayed (MY RULES, IPAD, COLLISIONS, and CONDITIONALS). When you select a block within one of these options, different menu blocks appear, such as:

CUSTOM

Go to center	Jump
Go to finger	Grow
Spin	Change color

CUSTOM blocks (multi-colored) are actions that you can make your character do.

MOVEMENT blocks (orange) will allow you to move your character on the screen.

MOVEMENT

Move Forward	Flip	Set Speed
Turn	Change X by	Set Angle
Set Position	Change Y by	

LOOKS & SOUNDS

Set Color	Set Size	Start Sound	Send to Back
Set Image	Grow by	Set Invisibility	Change Pose
Set Text	Shrink by	Bring to Front	

LOOKS & SOUNDS blocks (green) are used to change a character's looks.

DRAWING blocks (purple) allow you to draw objects using different colors on your program.

DRAWING

Draw a Trail	Clear
Set Trail Color	
Set Trail Width	

VARIABLES

Set
Increase

VARIABLES blocks (yellow) hold a number.

CONTROL FLOW blocks (blue) are often used to repeat instructions.

CONTROL FLOW

Check Once If	Repeat Forever
Repeat	Wait
Check If Else	Create a Clone

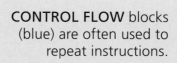

TITANIC
THE STORY OF RMS *TITANIC*

READY >>

The *Titanic* was the biggest and most luxurious ship in the world when she was completed in 1911. Her maiden (first) voyage was from Southampton, UK, to New York, USA, in April 1912. The *Titanic* had safety features that were supposed to make her unsinkable. Nobody could have predicted the tragedy that was about to happen on the night of April 14, 1912, when the ship hit an iceberg. In this project, you are going to recreate the sinking of the RMS *Titanic*.

1 **GETTING STARTED**

Find the Hopscotch app on your device and tap on it.

Tap on Create at the bottom of your screen. Tap on the Blank project lightbulb icon on the left-hand side of the screen.

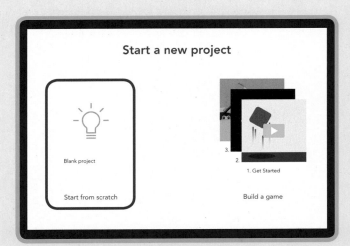

Start a new project

Blank project

Start from scratch

3.
2.
1. Get Started

Build a game

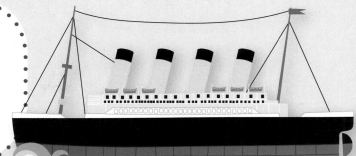

SET

Before you start coding, you need to set up the scene where your animation will take place and add characters for you to animate.

 2 ### ADD AND NAME OBJECTS

For this animation you will need four objects. Tap on the plus sign at the bottom of your screen. You will see emoji faces on the left-hand side under TEXT. Tap on the faces and a white box will appear.

Type "Sky" in the white box and then tap on the check in the green box. Tap on the plus sign again.

Add a second text and name it "Sea." Drag them and place them on the left-hand side of the screen.

When you drag characters on the screen you will see two numbers appear above your finger. These are called coordinates and they help position the character on the screen. Position the "Sea" on the coordinates (1001,187) and the "Sky" on the coordinates (100,585). Coordinates do not have to be exact; characters can be positioned close to those numbers.

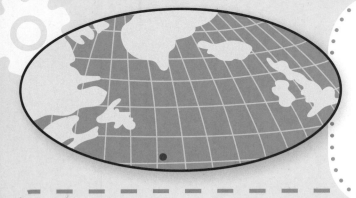

3 ADD THE ICEBERG AND THE SHIP

Tap on the plus sign at the bottom of your screen, go to SHAPES, and add a triangle.

Place the triangle on the left-hand side of the screen, at coordinates (50,500).

Tap on the plus sign again, tap on TEXT, and go to the TRAVEL & PLACES emojis and tap on the ship.

Place the ship on the right-hand side of the screen, at coordinates (1000,432).

Now that you have added the objects, you are ready to program your animation.

CODE! »

Now you are ready to make a program for your character. Use the colored blocks on the bottom of the screen to locate the coding blocks that you need.

4 CREATE YOUR BACKGROUND

Drawing a background is a skill that you can apply to any animation or game in Hopscotch. You can create your own background by using the purple Draw a Trail block in the Drawing menu. This block draws a colored path and the programmer needs to choose the color, width, and speed.

Tap on Add code next to the "Sea" character. Tap on iPad at the bottom of the screen and then tap on the block When Game Starts. Tap inside the red block and tap on Drawing and Movement blocks to set up speed and direction. You'll find these blocks by clicking on the three horizontal lines, top-right, opposite When Game Starts. Your program should look like this:

The Play box at the top right-hand corner will appear. Tap on Play to test your program.

Go to Edit, then tap on the See code box on the "Sky" character and add the following code:

When two things happen at the same time in programming, it is called a **concurrency**. Do the "Sky" and "Sea" work at the same time? Tap Play to find out.

The 500 width in this box will make the trail cover half of the screen. This will be the sea.

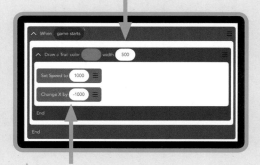

This block moves the object across the screen horizontally (along the x-axis). It has a minus sign because it makes the object move from left to right.

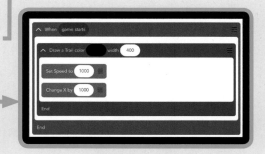

5 ANIMATE USING CUSTOM AND LOOKS & SOUNDS BLOCKS

You might have noticed that the triangle is black and a bit small for your animation. You need to fix that. Tap on the Add code box next to the triangle and add the following program:

6 ANIMATE USING CONTROL FLOW

A Control Flow block is used to control the action in a program. You need to make the ship wait until the background is ready. That is why you will be using a Control Flow block. Tap on Add code next to the ship and add the following code:

The ship should now move along the screen slower than the background. Tap Play to test your program.

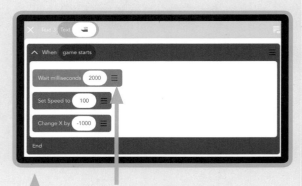

This Control Flow block in the ship's program will make the ship wait until the background is completed to move forward.

Did you know?

The night of April 14, 1912, was calm and starry. Suddenly, a massive iceberg loomed out of the darkness. The lookouts rang the alarm. First Officer Murdoch gave the order to reverse, but the iceberg scraped the side of the ship, cutting into the hull.

These two Movement blocks will make the ship look like it sinks.

In the Bumps block, add the ship to the first box and the triangle to the second box.

7 ANIMATE USING COLLISIONS BLOCK

A collision is a type of event, and in Hopscotch it is represented as When___bumps___. In this animation, when the ship bumps into the iceberg, the ship should sink.

Add the following code to complete the ship's program:

Tap on Play to test your program.

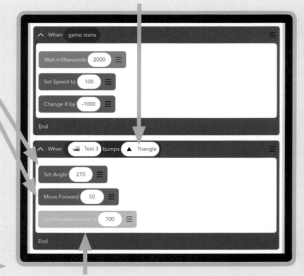

This Look block will make the ship disappear after the collision with the iceberg.

TROUBLESHOOTING

Did the ship miss the iceberg? That is because they are not at the same level on the screen. To fix this, tap on Edit and put the iceberg and the ship at the same level on the screen by changing the coordinates so they collide.

Did you know?

After the *Titanic* hit the iceberg, it took Captain Smith and Thomas Andrew, the ship's designer, ten minutes to assess the damage and realize that the ship was sinking.

CHALLENGE

Many survivors described the night of the accident as a starry sky with a full moon. Add more emojis, such as a moon and stars. Animate those using Looks & Sounds blocks.

BUSY AIRPORT

GET READY TO CREATE A BUSY AIRPORT SCENE

READY >

In this project, you will create an animation of a busy airport where an airplane flies by and another one takes off and lands.

1 GETTING STARTED

Find the Hopscotch app on your device and tap on it.

Tap on Create at the bottom of your screen. Tap on the Blank project lightbulb icon on the left-hand side of the screen.

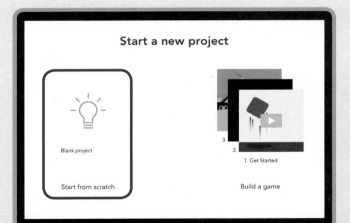

Start a new project

Blank project

Start from scratch

3.

2.

1. Get Started

Build a game

Did you know?

The first airplane was created by the Wright brothers in 1903. It stayed in the air for 12 seconds.

SET

2 DRAW A RUNWAY

Tap on the plus sign at the bottom of your screen. You will see emoji faces on the left-hand side under TEXT. Tap on the faces and a white box will appear. Then tap on the check in the green box.

Set text

✓

Using event blocks

An event is a trigger that makes the computer do something. You need to use an event to draw the runway.

Tap on Add code next to Text and add the following program. Tap Play to see the runway.

Tap the block Draw a Trail from the Drawing menu and drop it inside the When game starts block. This program will draw the runway.

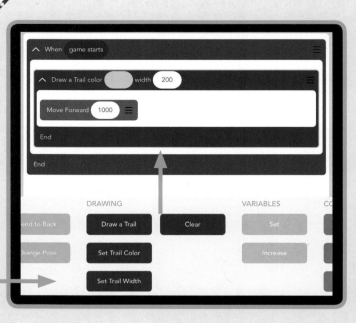

3

ADD OBJECTS TO THE ANIMATION

Tap on the plus sign at the bottom of your screen. Tap on the emoji faces on the left-hand side under TEXT.

A box will appear on the screen. Tap on the TRAVEL & PLACES emojis. Find the airplanes and tap on the green box with the check in it to add two of them to the animation, one ready to take off and one to land. You need to do this one object at a time.

Add a control tower from the same emoji section.

Place the airplanes on the left-hand side of the screen. Place one of them six squares from the bottom of the screen at (0,300). Place the other airplane three squares from the bottom at (0,150). Finally, place the tower on the right-hand side of the screen, five squares from the bottom at (1000,270). They should look like this:

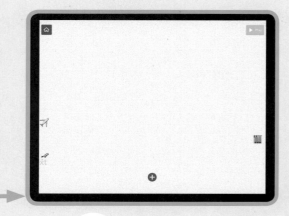

Now you have all the objects you need to program your animation.

4 MAKE THE CONTROL TOWER BIGGER

The control tower is small for this animation. You need to use an event to make it bigger.

Tap on Add code next to the tower and add the following code:

Tap on Play to test your program.

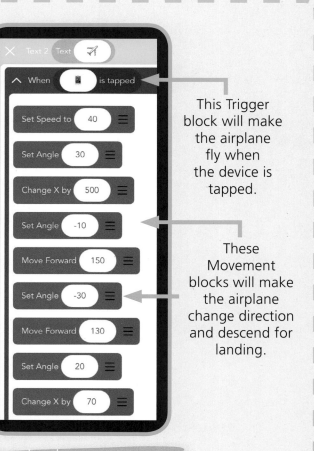

5

MAKE THE AIRPLANES FLY AND LAND

Now you are going to make one of the airplanes fly and then land by the control tower. To do this you need to use the Movement blocks.

Tap on Add code next to the higher airplane (0,300) and add the following code:

This Trigger block will make the airplane fly when the device is tapped.

These Movement blocks will make the airplane change direction and descend for landing.

Did you know?

The Airbus A380 is the world's first triple-decked superjumbo jet. It can carry up to 555 passengers.

MAKE THE AIRPLANE TAKE OFF, FLY, AND LAND

Tap on Add code next to the lower airplane (0,150) and add the following code:

Tap on Play to test your program. Remember to tap on the device to make the airplanes fly.

Set Angle blocks make the object rotate in relation to the bottom of the screen. These blocks will make the airplane change direction to land.

This block will make the airplane change direction to take off.

When ▦ is tapped

Move Forward 100

Set Angle 30

Move Forward 400

Set Speed to 50

Set Angle -20

Move Forward 200

Set Speed to 50

Set Angle -30

Move Forward 300

Set Speed to 50

Change X by 20

Turn degrees -45

X Text 3 Text

TROUBLESHOOTING

If you see there is a collision between the airplanes, it is because they are not placed correctly at the beginning of the animation (see Step 3). You need to ensure they are placed at the correct coordinates.

There are two ways to solve this and change the animation.

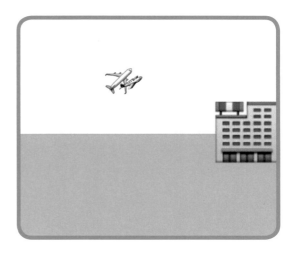

1. You can change the speed of the airplanes using different speeds in the Movement blocks.

2. You can use the Control Flow block: wait on one of the airplanes to make them move one after the other.

CHALLENGE

Use your knowledge of taking off, flying, and landing and add a helicopter flying around the control tower. Be careful not to crash into the airplanes!

MONKEY IN THE RAINFOREST

HAVE FUN IN THE RAINFOREST WITH THIS MONKEY GAME!

READY »

In this project, you will create your own video game. The object of this game is to make the monkey eat a banana before going to his hut.

1 GETTING STARTED

Find the Hopscotch app on your device and tap on it.

Tap on Create at the bottom of your screen. Tap on the Blank project lightbulb icon on the left-hand side of the screen.

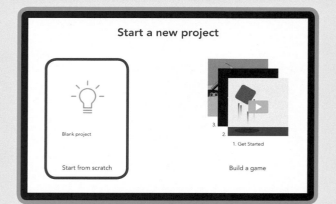

Start a new project

Blank project

Start from scratch

3.

2.

1. Get Started

Build a game

Did you know?
Monkeys eat fruit, nuts, flowers, seeds, and insects. For monkeys, bananas are a sweet treat.

SET

2 DRAW A BACKGROUND

Tap on the plus sign at the bottom of your screen. You will see emoji faces on the left-hand side under TEXT. Tap on the faces and a white box will appear. Then tap on the check in the green box.

Tap on Add code next to Text and add the Draw Background block. This is the only background available on Hopscotch. It is green and suitable for this game. Your program should look like this:

Tap Play to see the green background. It should look like this:

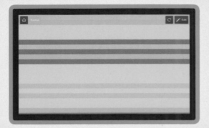

Did you know?

The New World monkeys of South America have tails that they can wrap around branches and hold things with. Some have a hairless pad at the tip of the tail to help with grip.

3 ADD CONTROL BUTTONS TO THE GAME

Tap on the plus sign at the bottom of your screen. You will see emoji faces on the left-hand side under TEXT.

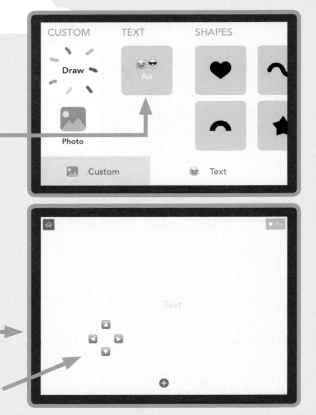

Tap on the faces and a white box will appear. Tap on the emojis keyboard. Find the up, down, left, and right arrows under SYMBOLS. Drag each of them and put them on the bottom left-hand side of the screen. Your control buttons should look like this:

Control buttons

4 ADD OBJECTS TO A PROGRAM

Tap on the plus sign at the bottom of your screen. Go to CHARACTERS, tap on the monkey, and place it in the middle of the screen. Next, go to JUNGLE and add the HUT. Finally, go to the FOOD & DRINK emojis and add a banana. You characters should look like this on your screen:

Now you have the background and the objects you need to program your game.

Did you know?

There are many different types of rainforest monkey, including Howler Monkeys, Spider Monkeys, Tamarins, Marmosets, Capuchin Monkeys, and Squirrel Monkeys. The most common monkey is the Tamarin.

CODE! ⟫

5 MAKE AN OBJECT MOVE

Now you are going to make the monkey move up when the up arrow is tapped. To do this you need to program the monkey. Tap on Add code next to the monkey and add the following code: To get to Text 2, tap on is tapped and and then tap on Text 2 in OBJECTS.

Tap Play to test your program. When you tap on the up arrow, the monkey should move upward.

```
×   Monkey

∧  When   [ ] Text 2  is tapped

      Change Y by  100  ≡

End
```

6

PROGRAM THE REST OF THE CONTROL BUTTONS

Add the following program to the monkey:

Tap Play to test your program. The monkey should move in the direction of the arrow pressed.

```
∧  When  [ ] Text 4  is tapped

   Change Y by  -100  ≡

End

∧  When  [ ] Text 5  is tapped

   Change X by  100  ≡

End

∧  When  [ ] Text 3  is tapped

   Change X by  -100  ≡
```

CREATE A RULE

A rule is a code that tells the computer what to do and when to do it. For this game, the monkey needs to eat the banana before going to the hut. You need to create a rule to make the banana disappear when the monkey bumps into it, so it appears to have been eaten. To do this, you need to add COLLISION and LOOKS & SOUNDS blocks.

Tap on Add code next to the banana and add the following code:

Did you know?
The word "jungle" comes from a Sanskrit word meaning "uncultivated land."

This COLLISION block will trigger an action on the banana when the monkey bumps into it.

This LOOKS & SOUNDS block will make the banana disappear after the monkey bumps into it. It has to say 100 in the box to disappear completely.

FINISH THE GAME

Finally, let's make the monkey go to the hut after eating the banana. Tap on the monkey, then tap on the plus sign and add the following code after the control buttons program. It should look like this:

Tap Play to test your program. Tap on the control buttons to move the monkey. He has to eat the banana first and then go to the hut. Have fun!

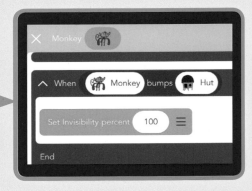

TROUBLESHOOTING

The numbers in the boxes in Step 6 may be different in your program. You do not need to worry about it. This number only shows the order you add the objects to your program.

Tap on this sign at the top right-hand corner of the program and you will see all the objects you added to your game.

When 🔽 Text 4 is tapped

Change Y by 100 ≡

End

CHALLENGE

Make the monkey jump after eating the banana.

Use a block from the COLLISION menu and a Jump block from the CUSTOM menu to make the monkey celebrate eating the banana.

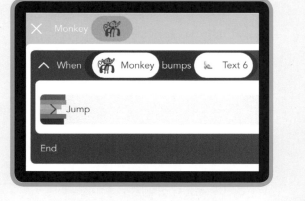

✕ Monkey 🐒

When 🐒 Monkey bumps 🍌 Text 6

⟩ Jump

End

LITTLE STAR

LET'S MAKE SOME MUSIC!

READY >>

In this project, you will create an animation where a piano plays the "Twinkle, Twinkle, Little Star" tune.

Did you know?

Music is created when sounds are arranged in an organized way. Music is made up of five main elements: pitch, melody, harmony, rhythm, and tone. If you create your own music—either by using real instruments, singing a song, or using Hopscotch—you will use these elements as you go along.

1 GETTING STARTED

Find the Hopscotch app on your device and tap on it.

Tap on Create at the bottom of your screen. Tap on the Blank project lightbulb icon on the left-hand side of the screen.

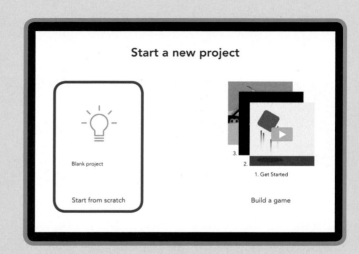

Start a new project

Blank project

Start from scratch

3.

2.

1. Get Started

Build a game

SET

2 DRAW

Tap on the plus sign at the bottom of your screen. You will see emoji faces on the left-hand side under TEXT. Tap on the faces and a white box will appear. Type in "Twinkle, Twinkle, Little Star." Then tap the check in the green box.

Place the text "Twinkle, Twinkle, Little Star" on the left-hand side of the screen at coordinates (234,400)

Tap on Add code next to "Twinkle, Twinkle, Little Star" and add the following code:

Tap on Play to test your program.

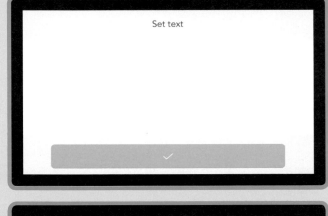

3 ADD OBJECTS TO THE ANIMATION

Tap on the plus sign at the bottom of your screen. You will see emoji faces on the left-hand side under TEXT. Tap on the faces and a white box will appear.

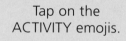

Tap on the ACTIVITY emojis.

Tap on the piano to add it to the box and then tap on the check in the green box

WEEEEEEEEEE!

4 ADD THE STAR

Do the same as you did with the piano, but this time go to the ANIMALS & NATURE emojis and add the star.

Drag the piano and place it in the middle of the screen and the star at the top of the screen.

The objects should look like this:

CODE!

5 ANIMATE USING LOOPS

A code that repeats is called a loop. Programmers use loops to tell the computer to do the same thing. There is a Repeat Forever block in the CONTROL FLOW menu.

You want the star to move when the music plays. Tap on Add code next to the star and add the following code:

Tap Play to test your program. Is the star turning?

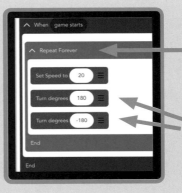

Repeat Forever will repeat the code inside the block until the program stops.

These two movement blocks will make the star turn right and then left.

Did you know?

Computers have sound cards that allow them to create and record sound. Until the late 1980s, most computers could only make a "Beep!" sound.

6 **USE SEQUENCE TO CREATE MUSIC**

In order to create music, it is important to make sure all notes are presented in the correct order. This is known as sequencing.

Hopscotch has a library of musical notes and sound effects that can be used in any combination.

To make music in Hopscotch, you need to use the Start Sound block in LOOKS & SOUNDS.

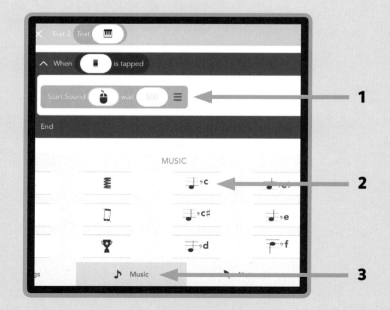

7 **ADD MUSIC IN HOPSCOTCH**

It is important to make sure that all musical notes are presented in the correct order. This is known as sequencing. Tap on Add code next to the piano. Go to Start Sound and follow these stages:

1 Tap on the mouse sign

2 Tap on MUSIC

3 Choose the notes.

Tap on the plus sign next to the piano. Now add the following code:

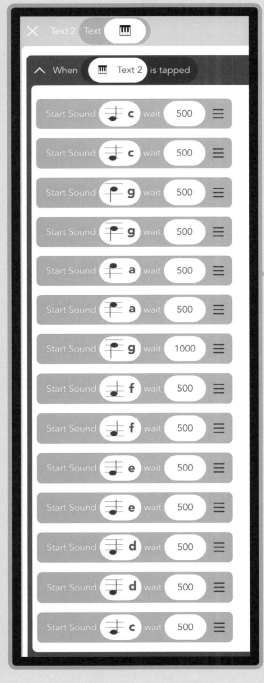

Tap Play to test your program. Remember to tap on the piano every time you want to play the music.

TROUBLESHOOTING

If the background plays very slowly, try changing the speed in the movement block.

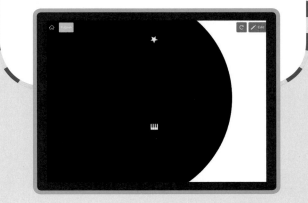

CHALLENGE

The "Twinkle, Twinkle, Little Star" text disappears when you play the animation because it is the same color as the background. Try changing the color of the background or the text and see what happens.

GLOSSARY

Animation
Something that moves around on screen and looks like it has come to life

App (Application)
A self-contained program that performs a specific function for end users

Character
A person or animal in a story

Code
A language for expressing information and instructions that can be understood by a computer

Coordinate
A set of numbers used to locate a point on a line, map, or grid.

Interact
To communicate or spend time with something

Interface
The way a computer program looks on screen; for example, the layout of the screen and the menus

Library
A collection of characters and backgrounds

Loop
A series of instructions that is repeated until a condition to end it is met

Program
A set of instructions in code that a computer follows

Sanskrit
An ancient Indian language

Sequence
The order in which instructions are given to the computer

FURTHER INFORMATION

BOOKS

Kids Get Coding by Heather Lyons and Elizabeth Tweedale (Wayland, 2016)

Understanding Coding with Hopscotch by Patricia Harris (PowerKids Press, 2016)

WEBSITES

www.gethopscotch.com

INTERNET SAFETY

The internet is a great resource, which helps you connect, communicate, and be creative.

However, you need to stay safe online. Always remember:

1. If you see anything online which makes you feel uncomfortable or unhappy, tell a grown up right away.

2. Never share your personal information, such as your full name, address, or date of birth, with anybody online.

3. Remember that people online may not always be who they say they are. Never share anything with people online unless you are sure you know who they are.

Note to parents

It is advisable to:

- Use filtering software to block unwanted content

- Familiarize yourself with the privacy settings of your device

- Set up passwords to protect personal information.

INDEX